I SURVIVED A SE(
EXTERMINATIC

Rudolf Reder

With a Memoir by Mark Forstater

Psychology News Press

First published in Great Britain in 2013 by
Psychology News Press
London

Copyright © Mark Forstater 2013

The right of Mark Forstater to be identified as the author of
this work has been asserted by him in accordance with the
Copyright, Designs and Patents Act 1988.

The author and publisher have made every effort to trace the
descendents of Rudolf Reder – and failed so far. In the light of the
historical importance of his testimony, they have decided to publish.
Any descendents should contact the publisher.

All rights reserved. No part of this publication may be reproduced,
transmitted, or stored in a retrieval system, in any form or by any means,
without permission in writing from the publisher, nor be otherwise
circulated in any form of binding or cover other than that in which
it is published and without a similar condition being imposed on
the subsequent purchaser.

Typeset by Keyboard Services, Luton, Beds
Printed in Great Britain by Biddles,
part of the MPG Printgroup, Bodmin and King's Lynn

A catalogue record for this book is available from
The British Library

ISBN 978-090-763337-2

Dedication

This book is dedicated to
my Zaydes and Bubbes (my grandparents):

Chiel and Molly Forstater
Anschel and Rachel Pincus

The publisher also wishes to dedicate this book
to his son, Reuben, a gifted writer too,
who died unexpectedly at the age of thirty-eight.

Contents

Part One	Introduction: A Perfect Killing Machine	1
Part Two	Rudolf Reder's Witness Statement	15
Illustrations		
Part Three	Memoir: Discovering Jewish Atlantis	43
Post Script: The Search for Zofia Reder		67
Bibliography		71

Acknowledgements

I want to give special thanks to my publisher David Cohen who has taken the risk of publishing this book, when I had assumed that it would only make its appearance as an e-book. For his courage and foresight I am deeply grateful. I would also like to thank Nigel Passingham for his publicity efforts.

I would also like to thank Feliks Pastusiak for his excellent translation of Rudolf Reder's witness statement. My old friend Richard Pepp read my memoir in an early draft and had many perceptive comments that I incorporated.

The audio of *I Survived A Secret Nazi Extermination Camp* is available on Audible.com, and I would like to thank everyone who helped me produce that audio: David Suchet for his fine reading, Jan Thornton his agent, the team at Heavy Entertainment whose recording and editing skills made this a painless experience, and Andy Statman and David Grisman for letting me use their moving version of Shalom Aleichem as the music for the audio.

Louise Brice and Laurence Howell at Audible have always been supportive of my work. I'd like to thank Tricia Kerr and Ruth Blair for their perceptive comments and suggestions on the cover design.

In Poland I have the following people to thank: Tadeusz Przystojecki of Theatr NN who was my guide to Lublin and helped me in my genealogical quest; Robert Kuwalek, of the Belzec State Museum, who always responded with valuable information about Majdanek and

Belzec; Joanna Krauze and Jakub Chmielewski of The Well of History were my impressive guides at Majdanek.

Without Jewish Gen I would not have been able to do the genealogical research that led to this book. I would like to thank in particular Stanley Diamond and Robinn Magid for their assistance. Robinn is part of JRI-Poland whose data I used in locating my Lublin ancestry.

Dr Robin O'Neil has been very generous in allowing me access to his extensive photo archive.

Finally, I would like to thank Joe White for putting together an excellent bibliography of Holocaust reading material. I hope this will be useful for readers wanting to learn more about this important subject.

This book is in three parts.

Part one – A Perfect Killing Machine – is a short introduction to the witness statement of Rudolf Reder, who was the only post war survivor of the Nazi death camp at Bełżec. The introduction gives some biographical information about Reder and some essential background information on the Nazi death camps.

Part Two is the actual witness statement made by Reder in 1946 to the Jewish Historical Commission. For the audio, this is read by David Suchet.

Part Three – Discovering Jewish Atlantis – is a personal memoir by Mark Forstater about how this book came to be produced.

PART ONE

A Perfect Killing Machine

If the Holocaust is one of history's most shocking crimes against humanity, then the most appalling example of that crime is found in the three death factories of Sobibor, Treblinka and Bełżec. These three 'killing machines' are perfect models of the Nazis' macabre combination of cruelty and efficiency. They were set up in occupied eastern Poland in 1942 with the express aim of killing as many European Jews as possible in the shortest possible time and with the least use of resources.

The first person testimony that forms part two of this book is [...] ho was brought to Bełżec [...] kill was kept instead as a [...] onths in the camp, before [...] 2 Jews managed to escape [...] mony is one of the fullest [...] es of death. His testimony [...] cal Commission in Cracow. [...] zi concentration camps, of [...] the three death camps of [...] e concentration camps were [...] ergen-Belsen, Dachau and [...] nsions of the Nazi prison service to deal with those resisting the new order – political prisoners and communists, gypsies, homosexuals and Jews – and to eliminate them through overwork, starvation and disease. They were work camps, where prisoner-slaves were driven to exhaustion as part of the war machine. Auschwitz was initially set up in this way, but later gas chambers and crematoria were added to it, marking it forever as a place of infamy. In the concentration camps, records were kept and prisoners were given numbers, branded on their arms. There was at least a slim chance of survival in the camps.

But in the three death camps no records were kept and their entire existence was a secret, since all orders setting them up were given verbally with nothing committed to writing. The Nazis understood that they were perpetrating a profound crime – the industrial murder of innocent men, women and children – and they did everything to keep this crime hidden. They placed these camps deep in the countryside, within dense forests, with few neighbours to see what was happening.

None of these camps existed for longer than 17 months, after which they were totally obliterated by the SS. The buildings and fences were dismantled and destroyed, the ground planted over with pine trees, and farm buildings were placed on the site to try to eradicate these places from history. Since no records were kept it's hard to say how many Jews were killed in these extermination camps, but estimates have been made that about 2 million Jews (and 52,000 gypsies) were murdered, in the most horrendous conditions. The average time of survival for a victim (and they were not prisoners, only victims) was about two hours from arrival by train to death in a gas chamber.

The details of what happened in those two hours, the inhuman conditions in the freight trains that brought these people to their slaughter, and the workings of these death factories is explained in shocking and hideous detail by Rudolf Reder, who lived through it. Reder was born in 1881, and was just over 61 when he was brought to Bełżec. He was a chemical engineer and before the war owned a soap factory in Lvov, Poland. Reder had a wife-Fanny-and three grown-up children: Bronislaw, Maria and Zofia. Zofia managed to survive the war, but all the others died. Bronislaw was deported from Lvov a week before Reder, and it was only when he arrived at Bełżec that he discovered that his son had been taken there and killed.

Reder was working in his factory when he was rounded up by the Nazis and taken to Bełżec. After the war he re-opened his factory in Cracow. This factory was later confiscated and nationalised by the communists and Reder was arrested. He later changed his name to Roman Robak and together with his new Polish wife – the woman who looked after him after his escape from Bełżec – he emigrated to Canada where he died in 1970.

Reder had a tough character that could cope with the horrors of Bełżec. But there were Jewish workers in the camps, often intellectuals, who could not endure seeing their friends and relatives killed, and who were sickened at having to burn or bury their bodies. Their only escape was suicide. Abraham Lindwaser was assigned the job of extracting gold teeth from the dead at Treblinka, and one night could face it no longer and decided to kill himself. He tied his belt around a roof beam in his bunk, and put his head through it to hang himself. But another inmate saw what he was doing, took him down, and lectured him, saying, 'that although the work was despicable, not only would we have to do it, but we would have to cope with it. We would have to make an effort so that at least someone would remain who could tell what was going on here...'

This was the role of the survivors, to be witnesses to the horrors that they experienced. And this is what Reder's testimony is for us today – a powerful indictment describing four months in hell. The extreme barbarity of the Nazis led to events in these death camps that were so bizarre in their cruelty that without these personal histories these events, in time, will begin to seem almost unimaginable, the stuff of grim fairy tales.

In 1975 Gitta Sereny wrote a book – *Into that Darkness* – about Franz Stangl, who had been the Commandant at Treblinka, and who was in prison in Germany at that time as a war criminal. In the book, Sereny tries to answer the questions: 'How could it have happened? How could men be brought to commit the acts that were committed? And how could the victims 'let themselves' be victimised?'

Sereny thought that the Nazis' murder policy and methods 'were unique and uniquely calculated. The killings were organised systematically to achieve the maximum humiliation and dehumanisation of the victims before they died. This pattern was dictated by a distinct and careful purpose, not by 'mere' cruelty or indifference. They crammed people into airless freight cars without sanitary provisions, food or drink, far worse than any cattle transport; they whipped up an hysteria at arrival; there was an immediate and always violent separation of men, women and children; there was the humiliation of public undressing, the incredibly crude internal physical examinations for hidden valuables, the hair cutting and shaving of the women; and finally the naked run to the gas chamber, under the lash of the whips.'

She asked Stangl, 'Why, If they were going to kill them anyway, what was the point of all the humiliation, why the cruelty?' His answer was 'To condition those who actually had to carry out the policies. To make it possible for them to do what they did.'

Sereny asked him, 'Would it be true to say that you finally felt they weren't really human beings?'

'Cargo', he said tonelessly, 'They were cargo.'

To achieve the extermination of these millions of men, women and children, the Nazis first had to commit spiritual murder on those they killed. Their victims had to be made to feel that they were no longer human beings, that they had been totally abandoned by any human feelings of compassion or tenderness, so that, without any hope or expectation, surrounded by hate and indifference, and reduced by fear and terror to the state of animals, or as Stangl put it – 'cargo' – they could allow themselves to be driven to slaughter.

But it was not just the victims who were spiritually murdered. Those who did the killing were also spiritually murdered, otherwise how could they become inured to such suffering, how could they – day after day, week after week, month after month – continue to kill defenceless men and women, the old and infirm, and blameless innocent children?

To hear Reder's testimony brings us closer to the reality of the Holocaust. To hear about the factory of death, to learn the details of the everyday process of turning living people into corpses on an industrial scale, gives us an insight into 'the banality of evil' that constituted the Third Reich. But how can we imagine what it must have been like to live through this terror?

Gitta Sereny came even closer to this feeling when she described a visit to Treblinka with her Polish interpreter, Wanda. She wrote, 'It was a bitingly cold day – in spite of fur lined boots my feet were soon freezing. After 30 minutes or so of walking around on our own Wanda and I came face to face among the trees. 'The children', Wanda burst out, with exactly the words which were dominant in my mind: 'Oh my god, the children, naked, in this terrible cold.' We stood for a long time, silent, where they used to stand waiting for those ahead to be dead, waiting their turn. Often, I had been told, their naked feet had frozen to the ground, so that when the

Ukrainians' whips on both sides of the path began to drive them on, their mothers had to tear them loose... Standing there, it was unbearable to remember.'

The Holocaust only became truly personal to me when I had children of my own. I remember one night when my first two daughters were lying in bed asleep and I was watching them breathing peacefully. The thought came to me 'there are people who wanted to kill them'. It was an upsetting thought, that there were people so deranged that they would kill innocent children just because they had Jewish blood.

The suffering of babies and children is achingly heart-rending. In Yitzhak Arad's book *Bełżec, Sobibor, Treblinka*, there is an incident described by Bronka Sukno, a survivor from Treblinka. He recalled, 'On the platform where the women undressed, three babies were discovered after one of the transports had arrived in the beginning of 1943. Their mothers had lost them in the mayhem as they were made to run to the gas chambers. Kurt Franz, (the Deputy Commander of the camp), picked up one of the babies, lifted him up by his foot, hurled him through the air and watched as the baby's head shattered against a wall.'

It's easier not to remember these things, easier to forget the suffering of innocent children, their mothers and fathers, and their elders. Life is more tolerable that way. Why should we fixate on this terrible past? It's easier to turn away than to accept that these horrific and unbelievable actions were committed by people just like us. And yet, we must remember, as distressing and uncomfortable as it makes us feel. Because it's only by the act of remembrance that we can give back to these victims some small part of the humanity that was taken from them. Their lives were ruined and wasted, but every act of remembrance, however small, creates a link between the living and the dead. We who are living owe it to those who suffered and died so needlessly; we must remember them, because to do so re-affirms our own humanity, and with that comes the hope that we will not allow such a crime to happen again.

PART TWO

The Testament of Rudolf Reder as given to the Jewish Historical Commission

Cracow, Poland, 1946

In August 1942 there was no separate ghetto in Lvov. A few streets were designated for Jews only and thus formed a Jewish district. It comprised several streets in the Third District of the city of Lvov such as Panienska St, Wąska St and others. Here we lived deprived of peace and under constant harassment. Two weeks before the 'resettlement', news about the impending calamity was already circulating. We were in despair. At that time we already knew what the word 'resettlement' meant. It was said that one worker had managed to escape from the death crew in Bełżec where, at the very onset of the death factory, he had been building the gas chambers. He mentioned that the 'bathhouse' was actually a building intended as a gas chamber. He also warned that none of the people sent there would ever return.

It was also said that one of the Ukrainians employed in the killing of Jews told his girlfriend what was going on in Bełżec. The horrified girl felt it was her duty to spread the news and inform the doomed. This is how the news about Bełżec reached us.

Thus the rumours about Bełżec turned out to be true, which we now knew and which made us tremble with fear. That is why for several days before August 10th you could see frightened people roaming helplessly around the streets of the Jewish district, asking each other: 'What can we do? What can we do?'

Two weeks before the 'resettlement', General-Major Katzman, the chief commander of Lvov and of Eastern Poland had started to issue work stamps for chosen factories. Some of the factories received their stamps from the police station in Smolki Square. Such 'lucky ones' were few. Most people were looking for a way to save themselves, either by hiding or escaping, yet practically nobody knew what to do or how to save themselves.

Then came the 10th of August. Early in the morning guards blocked all the streets leading out of the Jewish district. Squads of four or five Gestapo, SS and Sonderdienst troops, spread out every couple of metres, were patrolling the streets. They were eagerly assisted by Ukrainian militiamen, called askars. In the meantime, for a few days, patrols searched house-by-house, checking each and every corner. Some peoples' stamps were accepted by the Gestapo, but others' were not. Those who had no stamps, and those whose stamps weren't accepted, were forcibly driven out of their homes and not allowed to take a shred of clothing or a piece of bread. Then they drove these people into larger groups and anyone putting up resistance got a bullet in the head. I was busy in my workshop but I had no stamp so I locked the door and kept quiet, although I heard them banging on the door. The Gestapo broke down the door, found me in my hiding place, beat me over the head with a truncheon and took me with them. We were all loaded onto streetcars that were packed so tightly that we couldn't move or breathe, and we were driven to the Janowski camp.

It was already evening. We were gathered into a closed circle in the middle of a large meadow. There were six thousand of us. We were ordered to sit down and forbidden to stand up, move or stick out an arm or leg. A searchlight beamed down on us from some kind of tower; it was as bright as daylight. Surrounded by armed thugs, we were unbelievably squeezed together: young and old – men, women, children of all ages. A couple of accurate shots rang out as someone stood up; maybe he wanted to be shot.

We sat like this all through the night: in deadly silence. Neither women nor children wept. At six in the morning we were ordered to get up from the damp grass and form into fours, and so a long column of prisoners was marched to the Kleparowski railway station. We were surrounded by an impenetrable ring of Gestapo and Ukrainians. Not a single person could escape. They marched us to the station and onto the platform. A short distance from the platform a long cargo train was waiting. It had fifty freight cars. Then loading started; Train doors were slung open. The Gestapo were flanking us, two on each side, with truncheons in their hands; they were hitting the heads and faces of all the people boarding the train. All the Gestapo were actively beating us, so that each one of us had bruises on our faces and lumps on our heads. Women wept and children, cuddling up to their mothers, cried. Among us were mothers clutching babies to their breasts. Driven by the Gestapo, who were beating us mercilessly, people stumbled over one another. The train doors were high so people had to climb up while at the same time in the chaos people were pushing each other aside. Anyway, we wanted to hurry up too and be done with it. On the roof of each wagon sat a Gestapo man with a machine gun. The Gestapo were beating us and counting off one hundred people per wagon. Everything happened so fast that loading up a couple of thousand people took no longer than an hour.

In our transport there were numerous men, many of them employed, with various work stamps that should supposedly have made them 'safe'. There were very small and older children, young girls and women.

Finally they sealed the doors. Packed together into one mass of trembling bodies, we stood tightly, one person crushed to another. It was stuffy and hot; we were close to losing our minds. Not a drop of water, not a crumb of bread. At 8 am the train pulled out. I knew that the engineer and the stoker operating the steam engine were German. The train was moving fast, but we felt it was dragging. It stopped three times on the way. Probably those stops were due to the coordination of rail traffic. During the stopovers, the Gestapo would climb down from the roof and not allow anyone to get near the train. People were fainting from thirst, but they didn't allow compassionate people, who wanted to put a dribble of water through the small barred windows, to get near.

We rode further on, and nobody spoke a word. Apathetic, without a single moan, we knew we were on the way to be killed and there would be no rescue. We all had the same thought: how to escape; but there was no chance of that. The freight car I was in was brand new and the window was so narrow I couldn't have squeezed through. Yet in other wagons people must have been able to force the doors open, because every couple of minutes we heard shots fired at the escapees. There were no conversations, nobody tried to comfort lamenting women, nobody hushed crying children. We all knew we were on the way to a certain and horrible death. We just wished for it to be over soon. Maybe someone escaped, I don't know… The only chance of escape was from the train.

Around midday the train pulled up at the station in Bełżec. It was a small station with several small houses standing nearby. The Gestapo lived in those houses. Bełżec is located on the Lublin-Tomaszów railway line, in Eastern Poland. At the Bełżec station the train reversed from the main line onto a spur that ran for another kilometre up to the gate of the death camp. Near the station there lived Ukrainian railway workers and there was also a small post-office building. An old German with a thick, black moustache boarded the engine in Bełżec. I don't know his name, but I would recognise him instantly – he looked like a hangman. This man took charge of the train and drove it into the camp. The ride took 2 minutes. For four months I always saw this same scumbag.

The spur ran across the fields. On both sides was open space, with not a single building. Finally, the German who drove the train to the camp descended from the steam engine. Shouting and lashing out, he 'helped' chase the people off the train. He personally entered each wagon to check if anyone was hiding inside. He knew all the tricks. When the train was empty and checked, he signalled with a small flag and drove the train out of the camp.

The whole area between the station and the camp was under SS supervision. Nobody was allowed to trespass; stray civilians were shot at. The train arrived at the closed off yard, about one kilometre long and wide. It was surrounded by a two metre high fence made of barbed wire and iron fencing laid one on top of the other. The wires were not electrified. You entered the compound through a wide wooden gate topped with barbed wire. Near the gate stood a hut where the sentries sat, equipped with a phone. A few SS men with dogs stood in front of the hut. When a train arrived through the gate, the guard closed it and returned to his hut. From that moment the 'reception of the train' started. Several dozen SS-men opened the wagons screaming 'Los!' They drove people out with whips and rifle butts. The train doors were more than one metre above ground level. People thrashed by the whips had to jump down. Everyone – old and young – they had to jump to the ground, some breaking their legs and arms as they did so. Children were getting hurt, the whole mass of people were falling down – dirty, exhausted, terrified. Besides SS-men there were also so called 'Zugführers' present on duty. They were the Jewish supervisors of the camp's permanent Jewish death crew. Dressed normally, they wore no camp insignia. The sick, the old and the smallest children – those who could not walk by themselves – were put on stretchers and taken away to the edge of the enormous graves that had been dug out. There a member of the Gestapo named Irrman shot them and shoved them with the butt of his rifle into the grave. This Irrman, a tall Gestapo officer – a handsome, dark haired man with a normal-looking face – was a specialist in the killing of old people and little children. He lived, as did all the others, in a small house near the Bełżec station, all alone. They all lived without a woman or a family. He used to arrive at the camp early in the morning and remain there for the whole day receiving the death transports.

Immediately after the victims had been unloaded from the train, they were assembled in the yard surrounded by armed Ukrainian askars, and here Irrman gave his speech. Deadly silence prevailed. He positioned himself close to the crowd. Everyone wanted to hear him out, suddenly hope rose in us – 'if they are addressing us, maybe we'll live, maybe there will be some work, maybe after all...' There were thousands of educated professionals, a lot of young men in our transport, and – as in all later transports – a majority of women.

Irrman spoke loud and clear, 'Ihr geht jezt baden, nachher werdet ihr zur Arbeit geschickt' 'First you bathe, and afterwards you will be sent to work.' That was all he said, but everyone was overjoyed, happy that after all they would be sent to work. I remember Irrman's words, repeated every day, usually three times a day, for the four months I spent there. This was a moment of hope and delusion. For a moment people breathed a sigh of relief. Everyone remained absolutely calm. In total silence the crowd was marched further on, men straight along the square to a building which bore a sign in large letters 'Bade und Inhalationsräume' ('Baths and inhalation rooms.') The women went about 20 metres further to a large barracks measuring thirty metres by fifteen. In here the women and girls had their hair cut off. Girls with long hair were sent to have their heads shaved, while young girls with short hair went together with the men straight to the gas chambers.

The women entered the building not knowing why they were being brought there, so peace and silence still prevailed. Later on I saw that after a couple of minutes, when they were given wooden stools and lined up across the barracks, when they were ordered to sit and eight Jewish barbers – silent as a grave, moving like robots – approached to cut their hair down to the scalp with hair clippers, at that very instant they became aware of the whole truth. None of them could have any more doubts, nor could the men on their way to the gas chambers. Suddenly – without any transition from hope to total despair – laments and shrieks erupted – many women went crazy. And yet many of the women, especially young girls, went to their deaths calmly.

Everyone, except for a few men – chosen for their skills useful in the camp – all, young and old, women and children, all went to their inevitable death.

I was standing at the side of the yard together with the group that was left behind to dig graves, and I was looking at my brothers, sisters, friends and people I knew being driven to their deaths. At this moment when naked and bald women were driven with whips, like cattle to the slaughter, without any counting – faster, faster – men were already dying in the chambers. The women's hair cutting took more or less two hours, the same time as the preparations for the murder and the murder itself.

A dozen or so SS men used truncheons and sharp bayonets to drive the women to the building housing the chambers, and up the three steps to the gangway, where the askars counted 750 people into each gas chamber. Those women who didn't want to enter were forced by the askars who shoved bayonets into their bodies – blood flowed – and so they were prodded to their execution. I heard the doors slide shut, then moans and screams; I heard the desperate cries, in Polish, in Yiddish, the blood-chilling laments of children and women, and then one communal terrifying cry which lasted fifteen minutes. The machine ran for twenty minutes, and after twenty minutes all was silent. The askars slung open the outside doors, and I together with other workers – leftovers from earlier transports, without any badges and without tattoos – began our work.

We were dragging corpses of people who were alive just a moment before. We were dragging them using leather straps, to the huge mass graves prepared in advance, and the orchestra was accompanying us. It played from morning till evening.

After some time I knew the whole area well. It was located in a forest of young pine trees. The forest was dense, but in order to reduce the amount of light filtering through, some additional trees had been tied to existing ones. Thus branches over the area where the gas chambers stood were twice as dense. Behind the gas chambers there was a sandy road along which we dragged the corpses. The Germans covered it with roofing made of normal wire, on which greenery was placed. This was to prevent aerial observation. The part of the camp under the canopy of leaves was dark. Passing through the gate one entered a huge yard. The large barracks in which the women's hair was cut stood on this yard. Near the barracks there was a small courtyard fenced off with a three metre high fence made of planks placed tightly together, not leaving the slightest gap. This fence made of grey planks continued to the gas chambers. That way no one could see what was going on behind the fence. The building housing the gas chambers was low, wide and long, made of grey concrete. The flat roof was covered with tar paper and above it there was a second roof made of net covered with greenery. Three steps, one metre wide, without a handrail, led to the building from the courtyard. A large vase full of colourful flowers stood in front of the building. On the wall, there was a large and visible sign 'Bade und Inhalationsräume'. Through the stairs one entered a dark corridor, one and a half metres wide, but very long. It was completely bare – four concrete walls. The gas chamber entrances opened on the left and right side of the corridor. The doors were wooden, one metre wide; they slid open with a wooden handle. The gas chambers were completely dark, windowless and totally empty. In each chamber there was a visible hole the size of an electric socket. The walls and the floor were made of concrete. Both the corridor and the gas chambers were lower than normal rooms, not more than two metres high. On the opposite wall of each chamber there was a second set of sliding doors, two metres wide, used for heaving out the suffocated bodies. Outside the building there stood a small outhouse, maybe two metres by two metres, which housed 'the machine', an engine fuelled by petrol. The gas chambers stood a metre and a half above the ground, and a ramp ran outside the doors on the same level as the gas chambers, from which bodies were tossed to the ground.

There were two barracks in the camp to house the Jewish death squad: one for general workers, the other for skilled ones. Each barracks housed two hundred and fifty workers, and both barracks were the same. The bunk beds were on two levels. They were made of raw planks with a small tilting plank to lay your head. Near the barracks there was a kitchen, further on a warehouse, an administration block, a laundry, a sewing workshop and at the end comfortable barracks for the askars.

On both sides of the gas chamber building there were graves, both full and empty. I saw quite a number of already full graves, covered with sandy mounds. Only after some time did they sink to a lower level. There always had to be one empty grave in reserve.

I remained in the death camp from August until the end of November 1942 – it was a period of massive gassing of Jews. I was told by my few companions in anguish, the few who had arrived there before me, that death transports were most frequent in this period. They were arriving every day, without a break, usually three transports a day. And each train had fifty wagons, and each wagon was loaded with a hundred people. When trains arrived at night, the Bełżec victims had to wait in closed wagons until six a.m. On average ten thousand people were killed a day.

There were times when transports were larger and more numerous. Jews were arriving from various places, but only Jews. There was never a different group; Bełżec served solely for the purpose of killing Jews. Jews were unloaded from the wagons by the Gestapo, askars and the 'Zugführers', the Jewish supervisors; a few steps further, in the yard, where they were to undress, Jewish workers were already present. They asked in whispers 'Where are you from?' Whispered replies said 'from Lvov', 'from Krakow', 'from Zamość', 'from Wieliczka', 'Jasło', 'Tarnow', and so on. I saw it every day – twice, three times a day.

Every transport followed the same procedures as mine. People were ordered to undress, the belongings were to be left in the yard,

Irrman always gave the same deceptive speech, always the same one. And every time people cheered up at that moment; I always saw a spark of hope light up in their eyes. The hope that they were being sent to work. Yet, a moment later the little ones were wrenched from their mothers, the old and sick were tossed onto stretchers, men and small girls were prodded with rifle butts further and further along the path concealed by the fence, straight to the gas chambers, and the naked women were steered equally ruthlessly to the second barracks where their hair was shaved off. I could tell precisely at which moment they would all realise what was awaiting them and the fear, the despair, the cries and the terrible moans that mingled with the notes of the orchestra. Men rounded up with bayonets, and stabbed, were the first to be run to the gas chambers. The askars counted 750 into each chamber. By the time they filled up all six chambers, the people in the first chamber would already have been suffering for two hours. Only when all six chambers were so tightly packed with people that it was difficult to close the doors, was the engine switched on.

The engine was large, one and half metres by one; it was an engine and wheels. The engine roared when it ran for long periods of time, it ran pretty fast, so fast that one could not make out the individual spokes of its wheels. The engine was run for twenty minutes sharp. After twenty minutes it was shut down. The exterior chamber doors leading to the ramp were immediately opened and bodies were tossed down to the ground. They formed a huge pile of corpses that was a couple of metres high. The askars took no precautions when they opened the doors. We did not smell any odour, I have never seen any canisters of gas, nor the pouring of any additional agents – all I saw were canisters with petrol. Eighty to one hundred litres of petrol were used daily. Two askars operated the machine. Once however, when it broke down, I was called in, as I was known as 'der Ofenkünstler' ('the oven specialist'); I had a chance to inspect it and saw glass pipes which were connected to lead pipes leading to each gas chamber. In our opinion the machine produced either a high pressure that created a vacuum, or that the petrol generated carbon monoxide which killed people. Cries for help, screams, desperate moans from the people locked and suffocating in the chambers lasted for ten to fifteen minutes, horrifyingly loud, and they became gradually fainter, until, at the end, all was quiet. I've heard terrifying screams and cries in different languages, because there were not only Polish Jews. There were also transports of foreign Jews. French Jews were the majority among the foreign transports. But there were also Jews from Holland, Greece and even Norway. I don't recall a transport of German Jews. But there were Czech Jews. They arrived in the same trains as Polish Jews, but with luggage, well equipped, and supplied with food. Our transports were full of women and children, but the foreign transports brought mostly men and very few children. The parents had been able to leave the children under the care of their compatriots and thus save them from a cruel fate. The Jews from foreign countries arrived at Bełżec totally unaware, believing they were being sent to work. They were dressed smartly, well equipped for the journey. The German thugs treated them the same as Jews from the other transports and the system of murder was the same. They were dying in an equally cruel and desperate way.

During my stay in the camp some one hundred thousand foreign Jews must have arrived and they were all gassed.

When, after twenty minutes of suffocation, the askars opened the tightly sealed doors, the bodies were in an upright position, their faces as if asleep, unchanged, not even blue, with a little blood here and there from the bayonet wounds inflicted by the askars; their mouths were partly open, their hands clenched, very often clasped around the chest. Those standing near would tumble out like dummies through the wide open doors.

All the women were shaved before being murdered. They were herded into the barracks, and the rest of them had to wait their turn in front of the building, naked, barefoot, even in the cold and snow. Tears and despair seized the women. At a certain moment screams and laments would break out, the mothers pressed their children to themselves, raving in despair. Each time my heart broke, I couldn't watch this scene. The shaved women were ushered further on, so that others now stepped on the multi-coloured hair which covered the barrack's floor like a plush deep carpet. When all the women from the transport were shaved, four workers equipped with brooms made of rope swept and gathered the hair into one huge multi-coloured pile. The pile reached half the height of the room. They hand loaded the hair into burlap sacks and brought them to the warehouse.

The warehouse for the victims' hair, underwear and clothing was in a separate small barracks, some seven by eight metres in size. There the belongings and hair were collected for ten days. After ten days the clothing and the hair were loaded into separate sacks and a special freight train arrived to collect this loot. People working in the office said that the hair was sent to Budapest. This information came particularly from a Jewish lawyer from Sudentenland named Schreiber, who was an office clerk. He was a good man. Irrman had promised to take him away when he departed for good. Once Irrman was leaving for a short break and I heard Schreiber asking him – 'Nehmen sie mich mit?' (Will you take me along?). And Irrman answered –

'Noch nicht' (Not yet). This is how he cheated Schreiber who was surely killed with all the others. It was Schreiber who told me that every few days a freight wagon full of hair was dispatched to Budapest. Besides hair, the Germans sent out baskets full of gold bars.

On the path leading from the gas chambers to the graves, over a stretch of a couple of hundred metres, stood several dentists with pliers. They stopped each worker dragging a corpse, opened the mouth of the dead, looked inside, pulled out any gold teeth and threw them into a basket. There were eight of them. Mostly they were young men left over from earlier transports to do the job. I got to know one of them quite well. His name was Zucker. The dentists lived in a separate small barracks together with the doctor and the pharmacist. At sundown they brought the baskets full of gold teeth to their barracks, separated the gold and melted it into bars. They were supervised by a member of the Gestapo named Schmidt, who beat them if the work went too slowly. Each transport had to be done in two hours. The teeth were melted into bars one centimetre thick, half a centimetre wide and twenty centimetres long.

Every day the warehouse was emptied of valuables, money, and dollars. The SS men collected the valuables themselves, packing them into suitcases which were later delivered to the local headquarters at Bełżec. One of the Gestapo-men walked in front, followed by Jewish workers carrying the suitcases. Bełżec railway station was nearby, only a twenty minute walk away. The Bełżec camp – that is, the killing operation in Bełżec, was under the supervision of this headquarters. Jews working in the office said that the whole shipment of gold, valuables and money had been sent to Lublin. Lublin was the main headquarters with authority over Bełżec. Clothes stripped from the ill-fated Jewish victims were collected by workers and brought to the warehouse. There ten workers had to wash every piece of clothing very carefully under the supervision and whips of the SS-men, who divided among themselves any money found. This work was supervised by a special team of SS-men, always the same team. Jewish workers engaged in unstitching the clothes and sorting them couldn't pocket anything, and didn't want to. What use were money or valuables to us? We couldn't buy anything and we had no hope of staying alive. None of us believed in miracles. Each worker was searched very carefully, yet quite often we walked on discarded dollars that hadn't been noticed and we never picked them up. It was pointless, as they had no value for us. One day a certain shoemaker deliberately and openly pocketed a five dollar bill. He was shot together with his son. He went to his death happy, because he wanted to put an end to it. Death was certain, so why continue to suffer? In Bełżec having dollars served only one purpose, to die more easily.

I was a member of the permanent death crew. There were five hundred of us. Skilled workers numbered only two hundred and fifty, while two hundred of us were doing a job that didn't require any skills – digging graves and dragging corpses. We dug the pits, the huge mass graves, and we dragged corpses. The skilled workers, besides doing their own jobs, had to take part in this work. We dug with shovels but there was also a mechanical digger, which lifted the sand above ground level. It dumped the sand by the side of the grave, and formed a sand pile which was used for covering the grave when it was filled with bodies. Some four hundred and fifty workers were always busy with the graves. Digging one grave took one week. For me, the most horrifying thing was that they ordered us to pile bodies one metre above the level of a full grave and only then to cover it with sand. Thick black blood seeped out of the graves and like a sea flooded the entire area. In order to get to a new grave we had to cross from one side of the older grave to the next. Our feet sank in the blood of our brothers; we were treading on a mound of corpses. It was the worst, the most terrible experience.

Our work was supervised by the swine Schmidt, who beat and kicked us. If someone wasn't – in his opinion – working fast enough, he ordered him to lie down and gave him twenty five lashes with a horse-whip. He also ordered the punished man to count the lashes and, if he made a mistake, instead of twenty five he received fifty. A tortured man couldn't withstand fifty lashes; the victim was usually able to drag himself back to the barracks and would die the next day. This happened a couple of times a day.

Every day thirty to forty workers were shot. Usually the doctor supplied a list of exhausted men, or the so called 'Oberzugsführer' the chief overseer of prisoners, gave the list of 'offenders'. These lists resulted in the execution of thirty to forty prisoners each day. During the lunch hour these men were brought to the edge of a grave and shot. Also each day new prisoners, taken from that day's transports, were added to the roster of workers. The office kept records of the workers – old and new – and kept count so that the number of prisoners was always five hundred. But no records were kept of the victims from the transports.

We knew, for example, that the camp and death machine were built by Jewish prisoners. But there was no one left from that brigade. It was a miracle if anyone in the Bełżec crew could stay alive for more than five or six months.

The death engine was operated by two askar pigs, always the same two. They were there when I arrived and were there when I left. The Jewish workers had no contact with them nor with any other Askars. When people in the trains begged for a sip of water, the askars would shoot any Jewish workers who gave them help.

Besides digging graves the death crew had the task of pulling bodies out of the chambers, tossing them on a high pile and then dragging them to the graves. The ground was sandy. Each corpse had to be pulled by two workers. We had leather straps with a buckle, which we tied to the hands of a corpse. The head often caught on the ground, yet still we pulled. We were ordered to put the bodies of small children one over each shoulder, and carry them in this way. When we were dragging corpses we stopped digging graves. When we were digging graves, we knew that thousands of our brothers were suffocating in the chambers. We had to work like this from early morning till dusk. Dusk brought an end to the work day, as this 'work' was only carried out in daylight.

By three thirty a.m. the askar sentry, who had been guarding the barracks at night, was hammering on the door, shouting: 'Auf! Heraus!' Before we even managed to get up, that pig Schmidt rushed in with his horse-whip and chased us out of the barracks. We ran out holding one shoe in our hands or even barefoot. Usually we didn't undress to go to sleep, but even slept wearing shoes, since in the mornings we didn't have time to dress.

It was still dark when we were woken up, but switching on a light was forbidden. Schmidt roamed the barracks, hitting out right and left. We rose as wretched and exhausted as when we went to sleep. Each of us was given a single thin blanket with which we could either cover ourselves or spread on the bunk bed. In the warehouse we were issued old worn out rags; if anyone as much as sighed when he got his, he was slapped in the face.

In the evenings the light burned for half an hour, and then was switched off. The 'Oberzugführer' prowled around the barracks with a truncheon and didn't allow us to talk. We had to whisper to our neighbours.

The crew consisted mostly of men whose wives, children and parents had been gassed. Many managed to get hold of a 'tallit' and 'tefillin' from the warehouse and when the barracks door was bolted for the night, we heard on our bunk beds the murmur of the 'kaddish' prayer. We prayed for the dead. Then it was silent. We did not complain; we were totally resigned. Maybe those fifteen 'Zugführers' still had some delusions; we did not.

We moved around like people with no more will left. We were all like one mass. I knew some of the names of my companions, but only a few. It was immaterial who you had been and what your name used to be. I knew that the physician was a young doctor whose name was Jakubowicz. I also knew a merchant from Crakow named Schlüssel and his son, a Czech Jew named Ellenbogen, who was said to own a bicycle business, and also a renowned chef of a Carlsbad restaurant 'Brüder Hanicka' named Goldschmidt. No one was interested in anyone else. We were enduring this horrible life mechanically.

At noon we were served lunch by filing past two windows. In one we received a bowl, and at the other half a litre of barley soup, basically water, sometimes with a potato. Before lunch we had to sing songs. Before evening coffee, we had to sing as well. At the same time we could hear the cries of people suffocating in the gas chambers with the orchestra playing – and in front of the kitchen stood a high gallows.

The life of the SS-men in Bełżec and in the death camp went on without women. Even drinking-parties were all-male events. All the work was performed by men. This was the situation until October.

In October a transport of Czech Jewish women arrived. It brought several dozen women, whose husbands worked in the death crew. A decision had been made to keep several dozens of women from the last transport. Forty of them were assigned to work in the kitchen, laundry and sewing workshops. They weren't allowed to see their husbands. In the kitchen they peeled potatoes, washed pots, and carried water. I don't know what became of them. Probably they shared the same fate as all the others. These were all educated women. They arrived with luggage. Some even brought supplies of butter. They shared with us what they had. And they would help if someone was working in the kitchen or nearby. They lived in a separate barracks and had their own 'Zugführerin' (female supervisor). I saw them talking among themselves during work (as I was able to move around the camp maintaining the stoves). They weren't beaten as much as we were. Their work ended at dusk when they formed a line of twos for soup and coffee. Like us, they'd not had their own clothes taken away nor were they given any striped uniforms. Introducing identical uniforms for such a short time wasn't worth the effort.

Straight from the freight cars, dressed as they were, with long hair, they were sent to the workshops and to the kitchen. And, every day, through the windows of the kitchen and sewing workshops they watched the incoming transports of death.

Day after day the death camp churned with mass slaughter. The normal day was full of deadly fear and mass murder. Yet besides that, there were instances of personal individual brutality. I survived and I witnessed such things. In Bełżec there was never a roll-call. There was no need for that. Spectacles of horror unfolded there without any public announcements.

I have to tell the story of the transport from Zamość. It was around November 15th, when it was already cold, and snow and mud covered the ground. On such a rough day a large transport from Zamość arrived as had many others. It carried the entire Judenrat, the town's Jewish Council. When everyone was naked, as usual the men were driven to the gas chambers, and the women to the barracks for hair shaving. But the President of the Jewish Council was ordered to remain in the yard. As the askars herded the victims towards their execution, a whole parade of SS-men encircled the President. I don't know his name, I just saw a middle-aged man, pale as a corpse and totally calm.

The SS-men ordered the orchestra to come to the yard and await orders. The Orchestra, consisting of six musicians, usually played in the space between the gas chamber and the graves. They played without a break on instruments captured from the victims. At that time I was doing some masonry work nearby, so I could see them all. The SS-men ordered the orchestra to play the melody 'Es geht alles vorbei' ('Everything passes, everything goes by') and 'Drei Lillien' ('Three Lillies'). They played on violins, flutes and an accordion. This lasted for a long time. Then they placed the President of the Zamość Jewish Council against a wall and beat him on the head and face with canes tipped with lead, until the blood flowed. Among the executioners were Irrman, a fat SS-man called Schwarz, Schmidt, and a few askars. Their victim was ordered to dance and jump to the music while they beat him. After a few hours he was brought a quarter of a loaf of bread and forced to eat it by more beatings. He stood there covered with blood, indifferent, solemn, and I didn't hear him utter a single moan. The sufferings of this man continued for seven hours. The SS-men stood there laughing, shouting loud and scornfully 'das ist eine höhere Person, Präsident des Judenrates' ('this is a dignitary, the president of the Jewish Council'). Not until six p.m. did the Gestapo man Schmidt push him to the edge of the grave, shoot him in the head and kick him down onto the pile of gassed bodies.

There were other individual incidents. Shortly after I came to Bełżec, from an incoming transport – I don't know from which town (we weren't always able to establish where a transport came from) – among a few men one particular young boy stood out. He was a picture of health, strength and youth. He astonished us with his cheerfulness. He looked around and asked almost merrily: 'Has anyone managed to break out of here yet?' That was all it took. One German overheard him and this young boy, who was little more than a child, was tortured to death. He was stripped and hung head down from the gallows. After three hours he was blue but still alive. They cut him down, laid him on the sand and forced sand into his throat with sticks. He died in agony.

Sometimes incoming transports were larger than usual. Instead of the usual fifty wagons, the train brought sixty or more. Not long before my escape in November this happened, with the result that from one such overcrowded transport a hundred men – already stripped naked – were still left. They ordered them to help us bury the dead, as a Gestapo man had calculated that the death crew wouldn't manage to bury so many people in the graves. They picked only young boys, and for a whole day they dragged corpses to the graves. Naked in the snow and beaten, they were not even given a drop of water. In the evening the villain Schmidt led them to the graveside and started shooting them one by one with a Browning pistol. He ran out of ammunition with a dozen or more still alive. So he killed them one after another with a pick handle, until no one was left alive. I didn't hear any moans, I only saw that when lined up for their death they tried to cut in front of each other – helpless scraps of life and youth.

The camp was constantly guarded by troops of armed askars and a couple of dozen SS-men. Yet only a few of them were active. Some demonstrated their exceptional brutality on every occasion. They were all beasts. Still, some tortured and murdered while 'staying cool' while others took delight in murder: their faces beamed with joy. I saw how happy they were at seeing naked people stabbed with bayonets and chased to the gas chambers. They took pleasure at seeing the despair and downcast shadows of mostly young people. We knew that in the prettiest house by the station lived the Commander-in-Chief of the camp. He was an Obersturmführer whose name I can't remember, although I still try to recall his name in my memory. It was a short name. He seldom visited the camp, usually in connection with some event. This villain was tall, strongly built, over forty, with a vulgar face – this is probably what a born criminal looks like. The man was a total swine.

One day the killing machine broke down. Notified of this, he arrived on horseback, ordered the machine to be fixed and didn't allow people out of the airless chambers – he let them smother and die over the next couple of hours. He crouched down in a fury, shouting and shaking all over. Despite his rare appearances he scared the SS-men. When the Commander-in-Chief paid even a short visit to the camp, I've seen Gestapo-men and askars tremble with fear.

He lived alone with his orderly, an askar, who served him. Every day the askar brought him reports. The commander-in-chief and many SS-men had only occasional contact with the camp. They had their own canteen and a cook from Germany who prepared food for all the Germans. They were never visited by their families and none of them lived with a woman. They bred flocks of geese and ducks. People said that in spring they received baskets full of cherries. Crates full of vodka and wine were sent in every day.

I once repaired a stove at his house. Two young Jewish women, whose job was to pluck geese, threw me an onion and some beets. I also saw a peasant girl who worked there, but besides them there were only German orderlies.

On Sunday evening they brought in the orchestra and had a drunken party. Only Gestapo men, just gorging and drinking. They threw scraps of leftovers to the musicians.

The whole killing operation was supervised and managed by four Nazi criminals. It's hard to imagine more evil people. One of them- Fritz Irrman, a man of about thirty years old, the Quartermaster of the camp – was a specialist in shooting old men and children. He committed atrocities with an impassive calm, remaining inscrutable and silent, everyday repeating to the doomed that they were going to bathe and then work. A very scrupulous criminal.

A very different approach to committing atrocities was that of Oberscharführer Reinhold Feiks. It was rumoured that he was married, and the father of two children. He spoke like an intelligent man, but he spoke very fast, and if he was misunderstood, he used to yell at you, like a madman. One day, he ordered the kitchen to be repainted and the work was done by a Jewish Doctor of Chemistry, who stood on the top of a very high ladder just under the ceiling. Feiks ordered him to climb down every couple of minutes, and beat him across his face with his riding crop so that the Doctor's face became totally swollen and bloody. This is how he did his job. Feiks gave the impression he was crazy. He played the violin. He forced the orchestra to play the melody 'Highlander aren't you sad?' again and again until they were totally exhausted. He forced people to sing and dance while he made fun of them and beat them. A crazed beast.

And I can't tell which one was more hellish and cruel – was it Feiks or was it the fat, stocky, black haired murderer Schwarz (who came from a province deep inside Germany). He controlled the askars to ensure they were properly brutal towards us and that they were beating us strongly enough. He supervised our grave digging, which meant he didn't give us a moment of rest. Yelling and lashing he chased us cruelly from the graves to the chambers where piles of bodies waited for their trip to the deep pits. He herded us there and then ran back to the graves. At the very edge of the graves children and the old and sick waited staring with a crazed dull gaze into the depths of the pit. They were waiting for death. They were given a chance to look as much as they wanted at the corpses, the blood, and to inhale the stench of decay, before they were shot by the bloodthirsty Irrman. Schwarz was constantly beating someone. You weren't allowed to cover your face against his blows – 'Hände ab!' ('Take your hands away') he would yell and continued beating with delight.

Someone who took even more pleasure from his bestial work was a young Volksdeutsch, Heni Schmidt, who was probably Latvian. He had a very strange German pronunciation saying 't' instead of 's' (he said 'vat' and not 'vas'). He spoke Russian with the askars. He didn't like to leave the camp for even one day. Agile, fast, thin, with a face of a crook, always drunk, he raced around the camp from four in the morning till evening. He beat people, deliberately observing the victims' suffering and taking pleasure in it. 'He is the worst of the thugs' – prisoners whispered, and immediately added 'They're all the worst.' Schmidt always hung out at the places where people suffered the worst tortures. He was always present when the unfortunate victims were herded to the gas chambers; he would listen to the women's ear-piercing screams emerging from the terrible chambers and ringing in the air. Oh, he was the 'soul' of the camp, the most degenerate, monstrous and bloodthirsty. He loved to look at the utterly exhausted and pale faces of the workers returning to their barracks in the evening. He would lash each one of them on the head with his whip. If one of us managed to duck, he chased him and made him suffer. All these Gestapo-men, and less prominent others, were monsters of a kind. Not one of them was human, not even for an instant.

From seven in the morning until dark they tortured thousands of people in various ways. In the evening they would return to their homes near the station while the askars kept guard with machine guns. In the morning, the Gestapo-men were in full swing receiving the death transports.

The greatest event for the thugs was the visit of Himmler. This was in mid-October. From early morning we noticed unusual activity on the part of the Gestapo criminals. On this day the routine for murdering thousands of people took less time. Everything happened faster. Irrman told us 'Es kommt eine höhere Person, muss Ordnung sein' ('A VIP is coming, everything must be in order'). They didn't tell us who it was but everyone knew as the askars were whispering about it among themselves. Himmler arrived at three in the afternoon together with General-Major Katzmann, (the chief murderer of Lvov and the whole province), his aides-de-camp and ten Gestapo officers. Irrman and the others led their guests to the gas chambers, from where corpses were just tumbling out. These were tossed to a spot where a huge mound was growing, a heap of young and very small childrens' bodies. The prisoners were dragging the corpses away. Himmler looked on and continued to look on for half an hour and then departed. I saw the joy and the elated mood of the Gestapo-men, I saw how satisfied they were and how they laughed. I heard them talking about promotions.

I don't know how to describe the mood we lived in, we doomed prisoners, and what feelings we had as we listened every day to the horrible pleas of suffocating men and women and the cries of children. Three times a day we saw thousands of people on the verge of losing their minds. We were close to madness too. We dragged on day after day not knowing how we did it. We hadn't the slightest illusion of hope. Each day we died a little together with the transports of people, who for a few brief minutes experienced the torment of illusion. Apathetic and resigned, we didn't even feel the hunger and cold. Each of us awaited his turn, knew he had to die and to bear inhuman suffering. Only when I heard the children calling: 'Mummy! But I've been good! It's so dark! Dark!' – my heart, my heart was torn to pieces. And later we stopped feeling anything.

By the end of November, the fourth month of my incredible stay at the death camp in Bełżec was nearing its end. One morning, the thug Irrman told me that the camp needed sheet metal plates, lots of metal plates. At that time my face was swollen and bruised, and pus was draining out of my wounds. Schmidt had beaten me on both sides of my face. With a venomous smile on his face Irrman told me that I would be going under escort to Lvov to fetch the sheet metal: 'Sollst nicht durhgehen' ('Just don't make a run for it.'), he said.

I was loaded into a truck together with four Gestapo-men and a guard. In Lvov, after a whole day of loading the sheet metal, I remained in the truck with one thug guarding me. The rest of them went out to have some fun. I sat motionless and without a single thought for a couple of hours. By sheer accident I noticed that my guard had dozed off and was snoring. Instinctively, without a moment's hesitation, I slipped out of the truck while the pig slept. I stepped onto the pavement and for a moment pretended I was checking something near the sheet metal. Slowly I moved onto Legionów Street. The traffic on the street was busy. I pulled my cap down and, as it was night and there was a blackout, nobody could see me. I remembered where a Polish woman (my former housemaid) lived, and I made my way there. She hid me. I spent twenty months recovering from the wounds on my body. And not only wounds. I was haunted by images of the horror I had lived through. Awake and asleep I heard the moans of the tortured victims – and the cries of children – and the roar of the engine. I couldn't tear the faces of the Gestapo-men from my memory. Still, I endured until the liberation.

When the Red Army drove the German criminals out of Lvov, and I was able to walk out into God's world to breathe the clean air and to think and feel something for the first time since the German slavery, I felt the need to see the place where they had murdered two and half million people – people who just wanted to live, to live.

Soon I made the trip. I talked to local people. They told me that in 1943 transport became scarce and the centre of the Jewish killing operation was moved to the gas chambers of Auschwitz. In 1944 the pits were opened, the corpses were soaked with petrol and set on fire. Thick dark smoke rose and drifted for a couple of dozen kilometres around the huge bonfires. The stench and human particles were blown by the wind over far distances for a very long time: for long days and nights, for long weeks.

And afterwards – as the local citizens told me – the bones were ground up and the wind blew the dust over fields and forests. The machine for milling human bones was installed by a prisoner of Janowski camp, Spilke, who was brought to Bełżec for this purpose. He told me that all he had found there were piles of human bones – all the buildings had disappeared. He managed later to escape and survived. At present he is staying in Hungary. He told me this after Lvov was liberated by the Red Army.

When the production of 'artificial fertilizer' from millions of human bones was finished, the torn up graves were filled in and the surface of the blood soaked earth was neatly levelled. The sinister German monster had covered the tomb of millions of Jews in the extermination camp in Bełżec with lush greenery.

I said goodbye to my informants and started on the familiar path along the 'rail spur'. The rails were not there anymore. A walk through the field brought me to the living, fragrant pine forest. It was very quiet. In the middle of the forest there was a spacious, bright meadow.

THE LEADER-POST, REGINA, MONDAY, JANUARY 25, 1960

Survivor willing to give testimony

TORONTO (CP) — A Toronto man, believed to be the last survivor of a Second World War Nazi death camp, said Saturday he is willing to testify at the trial in West Germany of the alleged commandant of the camp where thousands of Jews were murdered.

Roman Robak, now 79, said he has notified court officials he is willing to give evidence but cannot afford to travel to Ludwigsburg for the trial.

Mr. Robak was traced to Toronto through a radio appeal from Haifa, Israel, where records at the Nazi war crimes census centre back his claim as the sole survivor of the horror camp at Belzec, near Lvov. The files there list him by his former name of Rudolph Reder.

2,000,000 DEAD

Official reports estimate the death toll at Belzec camp at more than 500,000, but Mr. Robak puts the figure at "well over 2,000,000."

His testimony now is wanted in the trial of Joseph Oberhauser, said to have been in charge at the camp.

It was only through luck that he escaped the gas chambers that killed his son Bronislaw a week before he himself was sent there, said Mr. Robak. He claims he saw 1,500 prisoners herded into the gas chambers daily. He was kept alive to build stoves in the buildings of camp personnel.

When his guard fell asleep, Mr. Robak said he walked away and hid for more than two years in the house of a non-Jewish Polish woman he had known before the war. Later he married her.

After surviving a typhoid attack as he lay in a small space behind a bookcase, Mr. Robak emerged from hiding when the Russians re-entered Lvov in 1944.

He and his wife Joanna came to Canada in 1952 and have had only occasional jobs since. The former owner of a soap factory, Mr. Robak recently washed dishes in a Toronto mission.

MAY TESTIFY: Roman Robak, 79, of Toronto, believed to be the last survivor of a Second World War Nazi death camp at Belzec, Poland, has said he is willing to testify at the trial of the alleged camp commandant but he can not afford to travel to West Germany for the trial. Joseph Oberhauser is said to have been in charge of the camp. Robak, traced to Toronto through a radio appeal from Haifa, Israel, where records have him listed under his old name of Rudolph Reder, said it was only luck that he ecaped the gas chamber which killed his son.

MISSING FISH

FALMOUTH, England (CP)— The white fishery authority will try to solve the mystery of the missing shoals of pilchards. Disappearance of the herring-type fish brought fishing and canning industries in this Cornwall seaport to a standstill.

Coast guard rescues man

PRINCE RUPERT, B.C. (CP) —A United States coast guard aircraft late Saturday evacuated a pleurisy victim from the Royal Canadian Navy frigate HMCS Jonquiere in northern British Columbia waters.

In hospital here following a 50-minute flight from Englefield Bay in the Queen Charlotte Islands is Petty Officer S. A. McCoy of Victoria.

Navy officials said his condition was reported by hospital authorities as serious.

The Jonquiere, currently on an independent exercise, did not carry a doctor. When McCoy's condition became more serious Saturday the navy contacted RCAF rescue centre in Vancouver for a mercy flight.

The rescue co-ordination centre said it could not reach the scene before dark and called on the U.S. coast guard, which had an aircraft in the area.

A Canadian article about Rudolf Reder

SS-Hauptscharführer Gottfried Schwarz.
(Photo: Dr. Robin O'Neil in association with Yad Vashem)

Stationmaster and train driver Rudolf Gockel.
(Photo: Dr. Robin O'Neil in association with Yad Vashem)

Photo found on a prisoner (from *Scourge of The Swastika*).

Ukrainian Guards' Bar.
(Photo: Dr. Robin O'Neil in association with Yad Vashem)

Administration and Armoury Building.
(Photo: Dr. Robin O'Neil in association with Yad Vashem)

SS-Scharführer Kurt Franz walking. Franz trained the Ukrainian guards.
(Photo: Dr. Robin O'Neil in association with Yad Vashem)

The Grodzka Gate, Lublin.
(Photo: The Archives of Theatr NN)

Ukrainian Guards.
(Photo: Dr. Robin O'Neil in association with Yad Vashem)

Warehouses at Belzec Station.
(Photo: Dr. Robin O'Neil in association with Yad Vashem)

SS-Untersturmführer Josef Oberhauser, SS-Oberscharführer Fritz Jirmann (Irrman),
SS-Scharführer Kurt Franz.
(Photo: Dr. Robin O'Neil in association with Yad Vashem)

Lublin ghetto.
(Photo: The Archives of Theatr NN)

Jewish Atlantis: the old ghetto streets are covered by the concrete Plaz Zamkovy. Lublin.
(Photo: Asia Zetar)

A group of Volksdeutsch, Poles of German descent, who worked for the Nazis at Belzec.
(Photo: Dr. Robin O'Neil in association with Yad Vashem)

SS-Hauptsturmführer Gottlieb Hering (right) drinking
– Commandant of Belzec mentioned by Reder.
(Photo: Dr. Robin O'Neil in association with Yad Vashem)

SS guards.
(Photo: Dr. Robin O'Neil in association with Yad Vashem)

PART THREE

Discovering Jewish Atlantis

A cool and windy Sunday morning in May 2010. I am in a taxi travelling from the city of Lublin in Eastern Poland to the Majdanek Concentration Camp, ten minutes away. This place where 80,000 people were killed (60,000 of whom were Jewish) is now a state museum. I am going there to meet two young Poles – Kuba and Asia – who are to be my guides for a tour of the camp. I was told to look for them near the old camp entrance, and as the taxi approaches the museum building I can see two figures looking anxiously out at the passing traffic: – a tall slim young man – Kuba – and a shorter reddish haired young woman – Asia. They are waiting by two large stones marking the walkway into the camp itself. I pay the taxi, greet my young guides, and we enter the camp. I didn't realise at the time how important this journey to Majdanek was going to be, and it was purely by chance that at the end of this visit I found the missing key to the interlocking stories that had been absorbing me. Every journey tells a story, and this short journey was no exception. It turned out to be a story that linked with a number of other stories in my life: that of myself, both young and old, the story of my grandparents, and, further back in time, the story of my ancestors. Through this missing key, these three stories became interlocked with a final one – one that I discovered at Majdanek – and it was this discovery that led directly to the making of this audio and book. I'm going to describe my journey, which I know will be familiar to many Jewish Americans of my generation, but I hope that it will also be of interest to non-Jews and to those much younger than myself.

Majdanek was both a work camp and a death camp, like Auschwitz, but on a much smaller scale. It was where many of Lublin's

Jews died, including, I am sure, some of my relatives. But most of my relatives probably died in the death factory at Belzec, which was the death camp closest to Lublin.

This was the first time I had ever heard of Belzec, and it's remarkable that a place of such historical infamy is still so little known. It was the first camp to be purpose-built for one aim: to murder Jews by gas on a shockingly industrial scale. It is estimated that 600,000 Jews were put to death there, with no records kept. The time from arrival in the camp to death was estimated at only two hours. This conveyor-belt of death was constructed with heartless military precision.

The three main death camps of Operation Reinhard : Belzec, Sobibor, and Treblinka, became the final killing ground in the Nazi plan to destroy European Jewry. After the Germans defeated Poland in 1939, they began to herd the Jews into ghettos in all the main cities such as Warsaw, Lodz, Cracow, Lublin, Lvov, and so on. Conditions in the ghettos were so dire that untold thousands died of disease and starvation. But the 'final solution' devised by the Nazis was that the ghettos would be emptied by 'resettlement' to the death camps, which were constructed in late 1941 and 1942. Rudolf Reder's experience of being driven out of the ghetto of Lvov and transported to Belzec exemplifies this action. The Jews from the ghettos of Lvov and Lublin were sent mainly to Belzec, but also to Sobibor, while those from Warsaw were sent to Treblinka and so on. In this way two million men, women and children were destroyed solely because they were Jewish.

I was born in 1943, while all this destruction was taking place. But I was born thousands of miles away from these killing factories, in Philadelphia, where no one was being terrorised. Mine isn't a unique story. It's typical of many baby boomers, those of us born between 1943 and 1960. My generation grew up after the war at a time of unprecedented material abundance, when American industry was intact while those of Europe and Japan were in ruins. It was a time of affordable housing, of cheap energy and food, when a working man could make enough money from his job to support an entire family, run a car and buy a house. Looking back at this time now, when there is such job and financial insecurity, when two wage earners are barely able to provide an adequate standard of living, when energy and food prices are spiralling crazily, and the stress of work-life juggling disturbs family life, the settled existence of 60 years ago seems almost dreamlike in its ease and peace.

Of course life was tough for those on the fringes – the blacks, the unemployed, the low skilled and disabled, but for the upper working classes rising into the middle class it was a time of increasing wealth and the expectation that the future promised even more.

My family had been in America for only two generations. My grandparents had all arrived in Philadelphia in the early years of the 20th Century, joining their relatives and *landsmen* who had arrived years and sometimes only months earlier. They travelled from the 'old country', my paternal grandparents from Poland and my maternal ones from what is now Belarus. Because I have found out so much more about my father's ancestry, I'm going to focus on them, since it was by following the trail left by my grandfather that I made that visit to Majdanek.

My Zeyde – it's the Yiddish word for grandfather-was born Chiel Forstater in 1885 in Lublin, Eastern Poland.

At 19 he left with his new bride Molly and elder brother Isaac to emigrate to Philadelphia. The year was 1904. For the benefit of employers who couldn't handle his name he anglicised it to Charles. He read and spoke Yiddish, the language of the Jews of Eastern Europe, and I'm sure he also spoke Polish. When I first became aware of him he would have been about 63 years old. He was a round stout man, with a big belly, clean-shaven with glasses, and he spoke with a heavily accented English. Although my Zeyde was born in Poland, he always struck me as quintessentially Russian. He was like a large round Russian bear. He hugged everyone, loved all his family, and his eyes ran with tears at the slightest emotion. He was a sentimentalist, and was constantly dabbing his crumpled handkerchief at his eyes. He cried with joy, to know that his children and grandchildren were all healthy and thriving.

I assume he had little education outside of that provided by his Jewish upbringing, but when I visited him in the mid-1960s, at his geriatric home, he was reading Melville's Moby Dick in English. I suspect he may have read Hebrew, but he didn't wear a yarmulke and I never had the impression that religion was an important part of his life. My father – Max – the first born, was certainly secular in his approach to Judaism.

For example, although I had a bar mitzvah at 13, my family was not a member of any synagogue, we never attended services, and our home was not kept kosher.

With no skills to barter, Chiel worked in clothing factories, sewing pockets onto trousers. He also sold clothes on South Street, in the heart of the Jewish neighbourhood. When he was broke, the family lived on credit from the local grocery store until he was earning again. Money was tight and he and my Bubbe Molly soon had 9 children to raise. They had produced beautiful children and then grandchildren. What I didn't know, and would only discover years later, was the pain that he must have felt at the cruel history that had unfolded in Lublin during the war, when his sister and cousins were killed by the Nazis. I never heard any of this, but it must have been a secret sadness that he carried with him.

I know that many survivors of the camps were reluctant to talk about what they experienced and this created difficulties for their children. The wonderful graphic movel *Maus*, by Art Spiegelman, explores this generational problem. But even in a family like mine, that was not aware of any concentration camp survivors, history was like an iceberg. On the surface was a little bit of knowledge and memory of 'the old country', while submerged was a vast amount of painful history of those who had remained behind.

Chiel and Molly lived in a crowded Jewish neighbourhood in South Philadelphia, and began to raise their family, which eventually grew to 6 daughters and 3 sons, including my father, Max. My mother, Dorothy, liked to tell the story of how she met Max. Her best friend at school was Mary, my dad's younger sister. Mary was like a female version of Chiel: a heavy-set woman, but overflowing with warmth and affection. She brought Dorothy (Dot to her friends) back to her home one day, and Dot was captivated by the atmosphere she found there. Here was a large family crowded into a tiny house, with little money for anything other than food, rent and heat, but the atmosphere in the house was lively, warm and joyful. This contrasted so strongly with her own home, where her father Anschel (who used the name Harry) wasn't interested in being a father at all. He liked to spend his time at the schvitz (the Jewish bath house) with his cronies, drinking and gabbing. Whenever he made any money, his friends got hold of it first and his wife and kids had to make do. Although her mother – Ruchel, or Rachel – was an excellent mother and homemaker, she had no support from her husband. The atmosphere my mother experienced at the Forstaters must have been part of the reason she married my father. She wanted the kind of love that she felt in that household, and she thought that Max would bring that with him.

In 1964 I went to England to study for a year, and when I returned my Zayde Anschel told me about his time in London's East End. He had been there on his way to America, and even 60 years later he remembered that good English beer could be bought for a penny a pint. I later found out the reason why he was in London. The story goes that in the old country (Minsk or Pinsk-no one was ever sure what town they came from), he had married my Bubbe and she gave birth to their first son. Rachel and the infant were sent to Philadelphia and Anschel was to follow soon after. But weeks went by and he didn't turn up. When weeks turned into months, they realised that a search party would have to go back to the old country to see what had happened to him. As he told it, what happened was that on his way west, he was waylaid, first in Paris and then in London, and since he always enjoyed hanging out with his cronies more than anything else, the bars, cafes and pubs were too tempting. So Anschel was doing a poor man's version of the Grand Tour, taking his time getting to the port that would reunite him with his responsibilities.

Anschel wasn't cut out to be a husband and father, although he did bring five children into the world. We were told he was a carpenter, and there was a set of rusty tools in the basement, but they never seemed to get oiled or used, and we never saw him turn his hand to any DIY projects. He certainly never worked as a carpenter but made money by giving powerful massages at the schvitz. His specialty was to share a bottle of vodka with his friends and then use the empty bottle as a massage tool. His friends thought the world of him, but his family had other opinions. My mother used to tell us that during Prohibition, Anschel had set up a still in a garage to make illegal alcohol, but was soon found out.

As a child, I couldn't help knowing that there had been an evil dictator called Adolf Hitler, that he and the Germans had killed 6 million Jews, and that he was universally hated, not just by Jews. My father was too old to fight in the war, but he signed up to work at the Philadelphia Navy Yard, building and repairing ships as part of the war effort. His younger brothers and brothers-in-law all joined the army and did their part.

But what did it really mean to me that 6 million Jews had been killed in Europe? Who were these 6 million? It was an impressive number, maybe too impressive. How could you get your mind around that many people, and how could you imagine their deaths? How could they kill so many? It was too big a number to comprehend – like wiping out the entire population of New York City. And why kill them? I couldn't understand why someone would want to kill someone like me – just because I was Jewish. All the Jews I knew were ordinary people – mostly easy-going, hard-working family people, jokey, lively, peaceful and harmless. They seemed a very unlikely group to want to kill. This knowledge was terrifying, but in an abstract way; it had an unreality that I couldn't bring down to earth. It all seemed to have happened very far away, to people who lived in a black and white world, in grimy ancient ghettos. Here in peaceful and plentiful Philadelphia, where I was surrounded by Jews who were riding the wave of post-war plenty, it seemed an incredible – even impossible – thing to happen. It was no wonder that everyone thought of Hitler as a madman.

It was when I was 13 or 14 years old that I really found out about the Holocaust. The first book I ever read about it was called The Scourge of The Swastika by Lord Russell of Liverpool. How did I come upon this book? It's unlikely that my family had it, because there were no books at home other than a few Readers Digest Condensed ones. There were no records either, apart from some ancient 78 Fox Trots from my parents' youth. Culturally my home was a desert. My father had to leave school at the end of his 6th year to go to work to help feed his brothers and sisters, and my mother had to leave after the 8th grade for the same reason, so although there was a traditional Jewish admiration for learning in the family, there was no actual learning to pass on.

It was at the home of my friends that I found books and records, since their parents had all been educated, had been politically active on the left, kept up with current affairs, read books, listened to music and visited the theatre, even if it was mainly for musicals. It was from these visits that I was introduced to a different level of culture, and began to appreciate that there were other ways to live. It must have been from one of my friends that Russell's book made its way to me.

Over 50 years later I still remember this book. Looking at it now, I can see that Russell covered many aspects of the history of Nazi crimes: the establishment of the police state, the ill-treatment and murder of Prisoners of War, the war crimes at sea, the murder of civilians in the occupied territories, the use of slave labour, the setting up of concentration camps, and the 'final solution' of the Jewish people.

Lord Russell of Liverpool, born 1895 and died 1981 (not to be confused with Bertrand Russell, the mathematician and philosopher), had interrupted his Oxford education to enlist in the British army in World War I. In 1929 he left army life and trained as a barrister, joining the Office of the Judge Advocate General of the Armed Forces in 1934. He served throughout WWII, and in 1946 became Deputy Judge Advocate, British Army of the Rhine. It was from this position that he became legal adviser to the British Military Courts during the extensive war crimes trials. Russell attended and was responsible for many of the 356 war crimes trials involving more than 1,000 war criminals. His book is informed by evidence, documents and statements from these trials. When he decided to publish the book, in 1954, his superiors were against the idea, and he had to resign his post in order to effect publication.

I must have taken in some of Russell's extensive information, but frankly I don't remember it at all clearly. What I do remember, and what struck me most strongly at the time, were the stark black and white photos illustrating the book, and one picture in particular.

The photos were of scenes that have become familiar now, but must have been shocking then: a mass execution of prisoners by rifle fire, bodies being burned in pits, bodies damaged by medical experiments, charred bodies, hanged bodies, bulldozed bodies, wagon-loads of bodies. But the bodies that struck me most, and which I remembered for over half a century, were of three naked women snapped running through a concentration camp yard, with uniformed SS men in the background watching them run. I see now that the caption on the photo says, 'From a photograph found on a German Prisoner.'

Photography in concentration camps was forbidden, since the Nazis wanted no information about these camps seeping out into the world. So this photo, which looks as if it had been folded twice to fit into a pocket, was a clandestine stolen image. Aged 13, and in 1950s America, this was a shocking and sexually disturbing image to me. I had certainly never seen a naked woman before, and if I had it would have been in a girlie magazine. Playboy had only been out for a couple of years, and images of nudity were much rarer than they are today. There couldn't have been a greater contrast than that of the air-brushed colour saturated nudes of a Playboy centrefold, and this gritty stolen black and white picture. Perhaps the prisoner who kept it hidden used it as a memento of the sexual life he'd been deprived of.

Why was this photo so sexually shocking and disturbing to me? I couldn't understand it at the time, but I now realise that this photo illustrates an essential aspect of the Nazi machine: the license given to their followers to satisfy all their primitive instincts with complete impunity. The SS men and Ukrainian askars who ran these camps were given the freedom to abuse, humiliate, torture, rape, beat, burn, destroy, and kill with no law or morality to check them. They were allowed and even encouraged to revert to the primeval, and this license attracted people who wanted to strip off the mask of civilisation to delight in the dark forbidden orgy of the illicit and prohibited.

* * * * *

When I was growing up I had little curiosity about where my Zaydes and Bubbes had come from, what the old world that they left was like, and what had happened to the families they left behind. I never really appreciated that they would have had close family who had stayed put, who never left their familiar shtetl, town or city. I never made the link between the crude photos and graphic descriptions of Nazi barbarism, with the uncles, aunts, brothers, sisters and cousins my grandparents had grown up with. As I got older, I understood that the people in these pitiful black and white photos, the people starving in the ghettos and being beaten in the camps, could be my relatives, and that the horrendous descriptions of bodies being gassed are the death agonies of people who share my blood. The journey that I have undertaken is not just a physical one, from the new world to the old, but is a spiritual journey as well. It has turned out to be a journey of resurrection, in which I have brought back to some kind of life those who were murdered, and have given a voice to those who were made silent. The life and voice may be mine, but people who did not exist for me ten years ago now find a kind of life in my memory.

I continued to have an interest in the holocaust and eventually produced two films that dealt with the subject: The Cold Room and Forbidden, both made for HBO. Both of these films were shot in Berlin, and I soon got a reputation as a specialist in European co-productions. Through a director friend, the late Paul Bartel, I met the Polish director Krzysztof Zanussi, and this introduction gave me a link into making a few Polish co-productions. I was amused to find that in the credits of one of the Polish films I was listed as Marek Forstater. I thought that with a name like that I was really turning back to my Polish roots. However, even though I was spending weeks in Cracow and Warsaw, during the mid to late 80s, I never took the opportunity to visit Auschwitz, nor did I consider making a visit to Lublin. I was still not interested enough in my heritage to make these journeys, and although it didn't bother me at the time, it now seems strange that I didn't take advantage of the resources I had then – a car and driver, production assistants, translators – who could easily have arranged a visit to Lublin.

What was it that finally got me interested enough to begin the search for my Zayde's family? I don't know. Perhaps it was time itself, the fact that I was moving into my 60s and with that came the realisation that if I didn't start to do this research, that perhaps I would miss out on the chance forever. I have heard that every family has one person who becomes the record keeper, the scribe of collective memories to pass on to the next generation. Perhaps that's my role.

But there was also a practical reason why I began, and that was the wonderful research possibilities offered by the internet. During a web search I chanced upon www.Jewishgen.org, a not for profit internet site that is dedicated to helping Jews re-discover their roots. Founded in 1987 with only 150 users, it now has over 700 active volunteers who contribute to the collection. Currently, JewishGen hosts more than 14 million records. Exploring JewishGen I found a large section of Polish records that had been compiled by Jewish Records Indexing-Poland (www.jri-poland.org). The JRI volunteers had been working for many years transcribing Polish town hall and church records from the 19th and 20th centuries, and providing these records of births, marriages, deaths and sometimes divorces to the database of Jewishgen so that they could reach a large audience. These records are like gold to researchers.

Starting with the name Forstater and the town Lublin as my references, I came across my Zayde's birth date and that of his brother Isaac and from that information managed to trace back in time to about 1800, to the first Forstater that I have found so far – David Ferszteter, my great-great-great-great-great-grandfather. From knowing only my grandfather, I now knew five generations more, as, in the words of the King James bible, David and his wife Rivka begat Hershel, who with Edla begat Solomon Moses, who with Elka begat Mendel, who with Marya begat Israel, who with Golda begat Chiel, my Zayde, who with Molly begat Max, my father, who with Dorothy brought me and my brothers into this world.

Somehow this pageant of parentage gave me the feeling of being less alone in the world. The Chinese, who have a long history of ancestor worship, believe that every child who is born is given the task of redeeming and fulfilling the lost hopes and expectations of the seven generations preceding him or her. This is quite a burden to place on anyone's shoulders, but it does mean that when life gets tough, you have the awareness that there is a horde of your relatives standing behind you, giving you support and help. This is not a bad feeling to have.

Of course I knew nothing about these ancestors other than their names and some dates, but slowly more details emerged from the voluminous records of Jewish Records Indexing, and I soon found that some of my Zayde's family were rope-makers, others metal workers, and that he had a cousin Chaim involved in property who'd been instrumental in founding the first modern hotel in Lublin – the stylish Europa.

Because my Zayde was an unskilled worker, and his brother owned a small grocery store, I had always assumed that all my relatives in Poland would have been workers of some kind. There were no family stories of Rabbis or sages, or any sense of a heritage that was other than mundane. So I was surprised when I found there was a branch of Forstaters in Bialystok, about 250 kilometres northeast of Lublin, who had a more prestigious history. There had been Henryk Forstater, who was a writer, economist and critic, writing for the Russian newspaper Pravda. I found a Dr Forstater, who was an intern in the renowned Jewish Hospital in Bialystok. During the Nazi occupation Dr Forstater (along with the other interns) was killed while remaining with his patients.

To bring my records up to World War 2, I started to look at the database of holocaust victims held in Yad Vashem in Jerusalem, the Museum of the Shoah. Through their database I located a number of my family who died either in Poland's ghettos or in concentration camps. This information helped me to link these victims with the birth and marriage records from JewishGen. Now I had amassed quite a lot of names and dates, but not a lot of structure. I felt I needed more information and help. So I asked one of the JRI researchers to recommend someone who knew about Jewish life in Lublin. This turned out to be Robinn Magid, of California, who is the Lublin Archives Project Coordinator for JRI-Poland. I asked Robinn if she could suggest a researcher who could give me some assistance. She said she could, and immediately announced that my name was very familiar to her; she said she must have come across it many times whilst doing her own research. The next day she sent me a list of descendants from the marriage in 19th century Lublin of one of her family – a Cygielman – with a Forstater. So it turned out that we were very distantly related.

Robinn introduced me to Tadeusz Przystojecki, who works for a community group in Lublin – the 'Grodzka Gate Centre – Theatre NN.' Tadeusz agreed to put my data into a family tree, and made some further research. It seems likely that the Forstaters of Bialystok and Lublin should be related (in fact, it is such a rare name that everyone named Forstater must be related) but we have not yet found the link between the two branches. It's good to know that if I ever decide to retire I'll have plenty of time in the future to solve this family puzzle.

Tadeusz and I have now found nearly 200 Forstater family members in Poland, and we have put them together in an impressive family tree. I was pleased that all of these previously unknown relations now had names, some dates and a little history. But the downside to this pleasure is to see how this flourishing family that my Zayde left behind was cut off so completely by the Nazis. This part of the research led to some dark places of the soul. Sometimes I had to stop, and just didn't want to carry on with the work, so dismal was the history that I uncovered. But it wasn't me who had to live this nightmare. I only had to read about it and think about it. On the level of suffering mine was trivial compared to what they had endured. So I continued with the work. In the end I discovered that only two of my extended family survived the war. The rest of this large family were dead by 1943. So my pleasure at gaining this knowledge is tempered by a dreadful catalogue of death.

I read this in the Memorial Book of Bialystok:

Hell on earth for the Jews of Bialystok began on Friday morning June 27, 1941, when the Nazis entered the city. Without delay, they streamed into the Jewish neighbourhoods, throwing grenades into Jewish homes and wounding many. With unbelievable brutality the Nazis dragged Jewish men from their dwellings, beat them over their heads and forced them into the great synagogue. As this august house of worship filled with people, it was surrounded by Nazi vandals. Armed from head to toe, they hurled grenades into the synagogue, which immediately went up in flames. Crammed with more than 2000 Jews, the synagogue burned for 24 hours until Saturday morning.

Many human tragedies took place in the synagogue inferno. No longer able to withstand the putrid smoke, a son, following the wishes of his father, hanged him with a belt on a menorah. In many instances, people slashed their friends' and neighbours' wrists in order to shorten their ordeal. While 2000 Jews were perishing in the fire, Nazi soldiers moved through the Jewish sections of Bialystok, hauling men out of their homes and shooting them in front of their wives and children.

This brutal story is one that was repeated with terrifying variations in every Jewish town and city in Poland. In 1939 there had been three million two hundred thousand Jews in Poland. At the end of the war almost three million of them were dead. Among the dead were my Zayde's older sister – Bella. She, along with her husband, their sons, daughters, and grandchildren all died. As far as I can tell, they died in the Lublin ghetto, at the Majdanek Concentration Camp and in the death camp at Bełżec. An entire Yiddish culture, which had thrived for nearly a thousand years, was completely wiped out in four.

* * * * *

Late in May 2010 a Polish producer, Wojtek Palys, invited me to come to Warsaw to discuss a possible film collaboration. I made sure our meetings ended on Friday, leaving me free on Saturday to take a train to Lublin, where I would finally meet Tadeusz and see the city that was home to my family.

I didn't really know what to expect of Lublin, but I was surprised by the flat sprawling city that greeted me at the station. Tadeusz met me, dropped my bags at the hotel, and then drove me to his office in the old town. The old town of Lublin was once a walled city on a hill, and it still has its two gates at either end – the Grodzka Gate and the Krakowska Gate. The Grodzka Gate is also called the Jewish Gate because it once separated the Christian walled city from the Jewish Ghetto which extended below and beyond it.

Tadeusz parked his car just below the gate, a couple of hundred yards from Lublin Castle (formerly a prison and now a museum). When we got out of the car he pointed to the lawns sloping down and surrounding the castle and explained that this was once the site of the ghetto, which had been there since the beginning of the 16th century. In 1943 the Nazis had taken the ghetto apart piece by piece and burned it before they left Lublin. The Communist regime that took over after the war just covered it with grass, as if it had never existed.

In front of the castle, below a series of wide and imposing steps leading down to street level, there was a wide piazza for walkers and cars, and beyond that a crescent of 18th century-looking buildings with shop fronts. Tadeusz explained that this area – the piazza and the buildings – had all been built over the main streets of the old ghetto, which had spread from this area all the way down to the river. In that direction had been the main synagogue, the famous Maharshal. Only a small plaque, placed near the site of the old synagogue, would alert people to the fact that this had once been home to thousands of Jews. There is no memorial at the site of the old ghetto to the many thousands of Lublin's Jews who died at the hands of the Nazis.

We walked through the imposing Grodzka Gate and entered a small door tucked inside the arch of the gate itself. This is the entrance to the Community Centre where Tadeusz works. Although it is called a theatre, there seemed to be little theatre work inside. Instead, there is a permanent exhibition of Jewish life in Lublin, including the photographic story of one boy – Henio Zytomirski – who was born in Lublin in 1932. Every year, on his birthday, his parents took his picture, and the last one in the series dates from 1939: an elegantly dressed young boy in knee-length socks. Henio never made it past 10 – he was probably killed in the gas chambers at Majdanek. On another floor they have constructed a large scale model of the old city complex containing the Jewish district. This takes up almost an entire large room and here one can see all the buildings and streets as they once were – the synagogues and yeshivas, the ritual baths, the butcher stalls and the market. The centre has also recorded thousands of hours of oral histories from Jews and non-Jews about pre-war Lublin, to insure that this important part of history would not be lost completely.

I wondered what had made this theatre transform itself into a Jewish historical centre. Tomasz Pietrasiewicz, who was one of the founders of the centre, explains that when the centre was formed in 1992, the gate and the area around it was a semi-ruin. He and his colleagues were unaware that the huge space they could see from the Gate's windows – the concrete piazza with its buildings and car parks – covered what he calls 'the Jewish Atlantis': the ghetto that had been covered over, like a scab over a bloody sore, just as the Nazis had covered over Bełżec. The same process of obliteration was at work, so that the people of Lublin had forgotten about their former Jewish neighbours, and were unaware that Jews had once constituted 40% of the city's population.

Tomasz and his collaborators realised that just to put on plays, to – as he puts it – 'propagate culture', in a place with such a terrible history, was irrelevant. This tragic spot, this annihilated concreted over ghetto, called out to them, and forced them to give this 'void' a reality. The murdered Jews of Lublin and their underground city would have to become a reality, to come alive again in the collective memory of the city. This was Tomasz' vision – that the reality of the place where they were situated had to be recalled in memory before they could do any real cultural or community work. And he understood that there was a deep abyss between the magnitude of the holocaust and the artistic means to express it.

Tomasz wanted young Lubliners to know what had once been

the reality of their city, and so he set about trying to commemorate and preserve the presence of the Jews of Lublin, and to catalog their annihilation. He has created a Theatre Of Memory. As a child, he had grown up near the Majdanek Camp, and he had felt the eeriness of the place without understanding anything about it. The large barbed wire spaces, the watch towers, the low even barracks, the stark building with the large chimney all stayed as diffuse memories as he grew up. When he was at primary school, history was taught by an older teacher. She told her class that during the Nazi occupation she had seen a little Jewish boy being led away to execution by a German soldier. She told the class that the little boy's hair turned white in minutes. This story stayed with Tomasz all his life.

I wasn't aware that Lublin was once a thriving political and educational centre. It was called the Jewish Oxford because of all the learned rabbis and sages who resided there. A Hebrew printing press had been set up as early as 1574. Lublin had been an important centre of Jewish learning: a huge yeshiva – a teaching school – had been set up as late as 1930. Between the two world wars, new Jewish schools and synagogues had been established, and there were Yiddish theatres, newspapers and books. A vibrant Yiddish culture thrived here, as it did in all the Yiddish speaking lands of Central and Eastern Europe.

Standing at the Grodzka Gate, looking out at this Jewish Atlantis, I realised something about my name. Whenever people had asked me about my name, I used to say it was probably German, and that its origin was from the time when Jews were unable to live inside city walls. So 'for stater' – meaning 'outside the city' – was how I guessed the name arose. But standing at the Jewish gate of Lublin, and looking down to where the ghetto used to be, I realised that this place was very likely the spot where my name came from. It must have been a Yiddish name, and it meant 'one who lives outside the city' – so I assume that my ancestors may have been among the first Jews to build a house just outside the Grodzka Gate, and who might have been one of the early settlers in the ghetto.

The Nazis invaded Lublin in 1939. At that time the city population was 33% Jewish. Soon thousands of other Jews, refugees from the war, all flooded into the city. The Nazis made Lublin a regional centre of terror, and the administration of Operation Reinhard – the construction of the death camps of Treblinka, Sobibor and Bełżec, was carried out from here. The Jewish population were subjected to the usual Nazi brutality: they were forced to wear the yellow star, their privileges were taken away, their valuables and property were plundered, they were forced to move into a ghetto. Soon living conditions deteriorated: too many people, too little food, too little sanitation. People died from disease, from starvation. People were moved into work camps, then transported to places like Majdanek and Bełżec, where they perished.

So my family's history in Poland ends in 1943, with a recital of death: death by starvation and disease, being worked to death, shot, beaten, burned and gassed. It's hard to face these heart-breaking events. There is a feeling of morbid voyeurism in having to confront these terrible experiences. No amount of new age waffle about karma, or that every experience is a learning experience makes any sense here. What karmic acts could these 6 million Jews have committed that brought on this horrible tragedy. What kind of learning experience can we take away from the pitiless fate or destiny that destroyed an entire culture? The propagators of The Secret may talk about similar vibrations attracting each other, but what Jewish vibrations could have brought this Nazi terror to their doorstep? If, as people today like to say, everything happens for a reason, what reason can we give to this senseless slaughter of infants and children and women and men?

The facts are unbearably grim, and it's hard to face them. Is there anything that we can learn from the Holocaust? Not good lessons I suspect. That ordinary people are capable of immense evil? That pity, compassion, and kindness can be almost completely eradicated in people, by being brainwashed through an ideology of hatred. It's no wonder holocaust deniers exist.

All I can do for those of my family who were lost is to say – I am with you in spirit. I take on myself, as much as I can bear, the terrible despair and suffering and heart break and pain that was visited on you. Although this is only a feeble gesture, I stand with you at the moment of your death, and create a living link with you. This is all I can do. It's not that I want to communicate with the dead or feel that my link with them is a two-way connection. It's only for us, the living, that such a link is important and has meaning. The dead are gone; their lives are lost, and there is nothing that we can do to make up for their pain and suffering. It is only for the spirit of those who are now living that this connection has any value.

* * * * *

The Soviet armies liberated Poland from the Nazis in 1943, and put a communist regime in power. They turned all of the concentration and death sites into state museums, the reason being that 'Poles had died there'. There was no mention that the overwhelming number of victims in these camps were Jewish.

The Jewish history of Lublin was obliterated. The ghetto was covered by concrete and grass, just as the Nazis had covered over Bełżec, Treblinka and Sobibor, to attempt to lawn over their crimes.

From 1943 until the communists were overthrown in 1989, this part of Polish history was not taught in schools. But from 1990 onwards, Jews started to return to Poland to visit the concentration camps, sites where their relatives had died. Young people in Lublin were surprised to see groups of Israelis arrive to visit Majdanek, to say Kaddish – the prayer for the dead – for those who were killed there.

This raised questions in their minds about what had actually happened at these places and a spontaneous movement of curiosity and a search for hidden truth led to groups such as Theatre NN wanting to discover the buried past of Jewish Lublin. They wanted to erase the collective amnesia that had eradicated the uncomfortable past.

* * * * *

On the Sunday of my Lublin weekend I made my visit to Majdanek. After introducing myself to my young Polish guides Kuba (full name Jakub Chmielewski) and Asia (Joanna Krauze), we set off on the diagonal path leading from the camp entrance to the barracks where prisoners had been housed. Kuba did most of the talking, in Polish, and Asia translated, but often she commented back to him in Polish, and after an animated discussion they would translate the results to me.

They explained that when the camp was in operation, this path had been paved with tombstones taken from Jewish Cemeteries. So the 60,000 Jews who were killed here trudged to their death stepping on their dead relatives. This image was like a detail from a macabre fairy tale, but one written by someone like Franz Kafka and imaged by Gustave Doré. It reminded me again of the Nazis' weird love of the diabolical. This combination of the practical – the need for paving stones – and the cruel – sourcing them from the cemeteries-had a nightmarish quality about it. There was something creepily artistic and fantastical about this concentration camp, as if a diabolical imagination had been let loose to create a place that had never before existed – except perhaps in the distorted imaginings of artists, writers or the insane. The crematoria, with its ovens, added to this sense of a truly grim real-life fairy tale, with its echo of Hansel and Gretel.

We walked and talked for about five hours, and I was struck by the immense knowledge and interest that Kuba and Asia (and their friends) had in the history of this museum. And this interest was not just about this place, but encompassed the entire history of the Jews in Lublin. They belonged to a group – The Well of Memory – which aims to research and keep alive the history of Jewish life in Lublin. This gave me great heart, for here were young Poles, non-Jews, who were on a similar journey to mine. My interest is personal and familial, while theirs is national and historic. Although Lublin has not yet built a memorial to its lost Jews, it seems to me that Kuba and Asia, Tadeusz and Tomasz, are all involved in creating their own living memorial to the Jews. I know that reality materialises from ideas and thoughts, so I have no doubt that from the minds of these young Poles a suitable memorial to the Jews of Lublin will be built one day. I hope to be alive to see it.

At the end of the tour, we came to the main museum building, which had a few books for sale, most of them in Polish. I noticed one slim volume with the title BELZEC printed in rough red letters on a glossy black cover. This was probably not the first time I came across this word, but it was certainly the first time I paid attention to it. I picked up the book and asked my guides about the title. They explained that Bełżec was the death camp nearest to Lublin. It was the first time that I had heard about this.

I bought the book and read it that night. It had Rudolf Reder's testimony in Polish and English, along with some historical material on the death camp. I found Reder's witness statement overwhelmingly powerful and painful. I later discovered that many of my relatives died in Bełżec, some of them no doubt at the same time that Reder was working there. He may have dug their graves or carried their lifeless bodies from the gas chambers. Given this connection between them and the link that I was making between the living and the dead, I decided to make this unique document more accessible to English-speaking readers and audiences. I hadn't expected that the key to linking the family stories that I was exploring would be found by chance in a concentration camp museum's meagre book collection.

Memory is in a sense a journey, a journey back in time. And the journey I have taken, besides the physical one from country to country, is also a spiritual journey in which the past and present have become joined in my living memory. Today I have extended my life in time and have brought back some of my family's dead to life, within my life. And I think this is a journey that has been good for me to make – good for my heart, good for my spirit and even for my body. I'm pleased you could join me on it, and I hope that one day you will have the opportunity to undertake the same journey for yourself.

Post Script: The Search for Zofia Reder

In his witness statement, Rudolf Reder describes his effortless escape from the sleeping SS guard in Lvov. He explains how he found refuge with his former housekeeper – Joanna Borkowska, who hid him for the duration of the war. When the war ended, Reder married her and they moved to Cracow to set up a new factory. But he ran into trouble with the new Communist regime that had installed itself in power. Seeing no future in Poland, Reder and Joanna emigrated to Canada where he changed his name to Roman Robak.

In various testimonies given from 1954–1960, Reder described the fate of his family during the war. His wife Fanny and his daughter Maria (born 1919) died but Reder never found out how. His son Bronislaw (born 1907) was killed in Bełżec, one week before Reder arrived there. His daughter Zofia (born 1916) and his son-in-law Leonard Schenker (born 1908) worked at the Jewish Hospital in Lvov. After Leonard was killed, Zofia went into hiding in Cracow. Where she went next is unknown, although Reder said that after the war she went to England where she married again and lived under the name of Smith. She was said to be living in Wembley in London, and was still alive in 1993.

All of this information was conveyed to me by Robert Kuwalek and Ewa Koper. Robert is the curator-historian at the Research Department of the State Museum at Majdanek, while Ewa is the curator at the Bełżec Memorial Museum.

Reder died in Canada in 1970, and I assume that his wife Johanna died there as well. I was curious to know if Zofia, his only surviving child, had perhaps had children in London. It was unlikely that she would still be alive but any children could still be living, and they would know the family history. So I started to research the names Zofia Reder and Zofia Smith but found nothing. There was no record of Zofia Reder in the naturalisation records at the UK's National Archives, and I could find no marriage, death or birth records that mentioned her. I did find a few people named Reder but not Zofia. Naturally I did locate a few Zofia Smiths, since the name Smith is so prevalent, but again these were not the former Zofia Reder. We also checked the obituary section of the Jewish Chronicle to see if her death had been noted, but again the trail was cold.

This was frustrating, since it would be really interesting to me to find out what had happened to Zofia, and how she had survived the war. So I went back to Robert Kuwalek and asked him if he had any other details of her whereabouts in London. He told me that a contact of his had been in touch with Zofia in 1993, and might still have her old phone number. This could help, since with that number I could locate the area where she lived, and find if she was listed on the Electoral Register.

Robert reported back that his friend could not locate the number, but that Reder in his 1960 deposition to the War Crimes prosecutor had mentioned that Zofia was living at 18 Baxford Road in Wembley. I googled Baxford Road and could not find it, but there was a Paxford Road in Wembley, so at last I had something solid, a little nugget of information that might open up this search. I went to the Brent Archives and started looking at the Electoral Registers for Paxford

Road. There was no mention of Zofia Smith living there in 1993 so I went back to 1960, and there she was:

   18 Paxford Road Zofia Schmidt

Obviously the reason I had such difficulty finding her was that her new married name was Schmidt and not Smith. So I once again started searching for birth, marriage and death notices for Zofia Schmidt. And once more I came up with very little. The only death notice I found was for a Zofia Schmidt who died in 1997, so this could be her, as she was alive in 1993. However the death took place in Leicester, not London, and it listed her birth date as 1906 (when the information I had was 1916). I ordered a copy of Zofia's death certificate and unfortunately it did not give her maiden name, but it did give the name of the niece who reported the death. Through the Peoplefinder website I found her phone number and she explained to me that Zofia was an adopted aunt, had never been married and that Schmidt was her maiden name. So this was not the Zofia Schmidt that I was seeking.

  The search continues...

Bibliography

Yitzhak Arad, *Belzec, Sobibor, Treblinka*, Indiana University Press, 1987

J. Caplan, ed., *Nazi Germany* (Short Oxford History of Germany), Oxford University Press, 2008

Martin Gilbert, *The Holocaust*, HarperCollins, 1989

Raul Hilberg, *The Destruction of the European Jews*, 3rd revised edition, Yale University Press, 2003

Raul Hilberg, *Perpetrators, Victims, Bystanders*, Harper Perennial, 1993

Ian Kershaw, *Hitler* (2 volumes), Norton, 2000

Arno J. Mayer, *Why Did the Heavens Not Darken?* Pantheon, 1990

Michael Novick, *The Holocaust in American Life*, Houghton Mifflin, 1999

Lord Russell of Liverpool, *The Scourge Of The Swastika*, Ballantine, 1956

Gitta Sereny, *Into That Darkness*, Andre Deutsch, 1974

Art Spiegelman, *Maus*, Pantheon Books, 1991